CW00411069

EROTIC
Foreplay

EROTIC
Foreplay

Linda Sonntag

hamlyn

This edition first published in
Great Britain in 2005 by
Hamlyn, a division of Octopus
Publishing Group Ltd
2–4 Heron Quays,
London E14 4JP

Copyright © Octopus Publishing
Group Ltd 2003, 2005

ISBN 0 600 61265 1
EAN 9780600612650
A CIP catalogue record for this
book is available from the British
Library

Printed and bound in Hong Kong

The material in this book has
been adapted from *Sex Games*
previously published by Hamlyn

Warning
With the prevalence of AIDS and
other sexually transmitted
diseases, if you do not practise
safe sex you are risking the health
of you and your partner.

10 9 8 7 6 5 4 3 2 1

CONTENTS

INTRODUCTION

All too often sex can be a no-frills fast track to orgasm. While there are undoubtedly times when such an approach is desirable, deviating from your usual routine in favour of a slow and delicious exploration of your lover instead can breathe fresh life into your relationship (or guarantee to get a new one off to a flying start).

Explore imaginative and erotic touching to learn anew how to seduce and arouse each other. Take turns to give a sensual whole-body massage which, as well as being incredibly relaxing, can also be full of surprises and an effective way of opening the door to total body sensation.

Use these simple, stunningly effective foreplay techniques to spice things up and rediscover your own sensuality and sense of fun – and that of the person you fell in love with.

Warm up for sex

An erotic massage sequence that treats the whole body is a relaxing way to de-stress and tune into one another without words. It allows you to discover and enjoy parts of each other that you may never have explored before. Skimming unexpectedly over the usual erogenous zones builds erotic anticipation, passing intense feeling on to the next part, and turning your whole body into a finely tuned pleasure zone.

THE POWER OF TOUCH

Touch is the most intimate form of communication and massage is the oldest form of healing. A loving massage signifies total acceptance of his (or her) body, transmits affirmation and boosts self-esteem. A massage will touch the emotions as much as it touches the body and will help to get rid of both mental and physical stress.

Massage can ease tension and eliminate toxins from the body tissues caused by the stress of a working day. Once he is fully relaxed you can turn your attention to his erogenous zones.

THE GENTLE APPROACH

Massage eases tension and eliminates toxins from the tissues far more effectively than alcohol, tobacco or other drugs, which can gradually numb and depress the feelings.

When your partner is sufficiently calm, seat him down and begin a gentle massage of the back of the neck and shoulders. If you get a good reaction, suggest a full massage for later.

SYMPTOMS OF STRESS

These are the symptoms of stress to look out for:

- Looking dishevelled and exhausted
- Continual stretching and rubbing to ease aches in shoulders, neck and back
- Argumentativeness, frustration and aggressive repetition of parts of conversations
- Being clumsy and unable to concentrate
- Short fused and intolerant of small inconveniences
- Negative body language – continual pacing, tapping feet or drumming fingers
- Bad posture – either wound up with legs twined around each other, or completely slumped in a heap

MASSAGE TIPS

- Remove jewellery and keep nails short and smooth
- Make sure your partner is warm enough. Cover the part of the body you are not working on
- Use massage oil to lubricate their skin
- Warm the oil in your hands first – don't pour it directly on to the skin
- Be gentle and try to keep at least one hand on the body at all times
- Discourage conversation

HANDWORK

The laying on of hands is comforting, reassuring, calming and healing. To achieve the best effects, you need to learn four basic massage strokes: gliding, kneading, deep pressure and percussion.

TECHNIQUE 1: GLIDING

Glide your hands smoothly and rhythmically over your partner's skin. This soothing stroke is ideal to use at the beginning and end of a session: the broad strokes 'join up' the body after you have worked on specific areas.

1 Vary the firmness and speed of your strokes, and experiment with applying most pressure from the heels or palms of your hands.

2 Draw wavy lines on your partner's skin, opening out and closing your fingers.

3 Try a light pressure with the fingertips. This is quite difficult to do without tickling, so wait until your partner is fully relaxed.

4 Use alternate strokes – let one hand follow the other, skimming across the skin as if you were brushing crumbs towards yourself.

5 Make big circles with your hands, letting one hand follow the other. This is a very good stroke for centring the body and banishing mental stress.

6 Kneeling at your partner's head, glide both your hands down the back together, pushing quite firmly, then draw them up again.

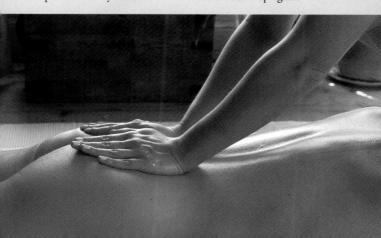

TECHNIQUE 2: KNEADING

This is a vigorous stroke and one that gives instant relief, transforming the body under your hands from sluggish and fatigued to light and energetic. The key lies in rhythmic repetition, which builds up a momentum that is almost hypnotic.

1 Choose a fleshy area on which to practise, such as the buttocks. Put your palms flat on your partner's body with fingers together and your hands pointing at 45° towards each other.

2 Make small circles with your hands, moving them up and outwards in turn, following each other.

3 Now add the thumb movement – every time your hand moves up and out, your thumb moves separately behind it, grasping the flesh and pushing it firmly along, as if you were kneading bread. You can feel the tensed

- One-handed percussion: as your left hand glides over your partner's skin, pound it repeatedly with the weight of your right fist (or the other way round).
- Two-handed percussion: keep up a loose drumming rhythm, working with alternate fists. Work lightly on sensitive areas, trying percussion with the tips of your index fingers.
- Hacking: work with palms facing each other, hands flat, fingers together. This technique is good for use on the buttocks, thighs and calves, but it could be painful elsewhere.

THE BACK

The expressions 'pain in the neck', 'I took it in the neck' and 'it really got my back up' are very revealing about the body's major stress sites. The back and the neck have everything to do with how we hold ourselves – and how we protect and defend ourselves from the rest of the world. The more problems or pressure in our lives, the greater the tension that accumulates in these key areas. Massage is a great way to observe your partner's body and to tune in to each before there is any pressure to perform. Stress and fear are the enemies of sex, so the first thing you need to do for a stressed-out partner is rub her back. Here's how to massage the back, neck and shoulders properly to release those hard knots of tension that are ruining her mood.

SEXUAL TENSION BUSTER 1

1 Kneel astride your partner's buttocks for a position of warm intimate contact. Begin by leaning forwards and working on the base of the neck with firm pressure and small deep kneading strokes. Use your the thumbs and fingers and really lose yourself, allowing the knots of tension you can feel to dictate your movements. Try to become invisible, existing only in the intuitive movements of your hands.

2 Move to your partner's side so that you can work the shoulder nearest you comfortably. Using fine and detailed pressure with the

fingers and thumbs, feel your way round the contours of the shoulder blade, smoothing out any grittiness as you go. Lift the shoulder and rotate it, continuing to work the flesh with the other hand. When you have finished change sides, keeping one hand gently on your partner's body all the time and repeat the movements on the other shoulder.

3 Straddle your partner again and work up and down the back with broad gliding strokes, pushing the flesh towards the neck under your hands, then dragging your palms back down with splayed fingers trailing.

4 Repeat several times, then work a thumb's width down either side of the spine, using walking steps with your fingers and thumbs and wiggling them in minute circles where they land. Don't touch your partner's spine with anything but the lightest touch, as contact here can be uncomfortable.

5 Finish the back massage with broad sensual gliding stokes that go up the centre of the back and sweep down the sides together.

6 Straddling your partner's legs without putting pressure on them, move on to the buttocks. Use vigorous kneading strokes, or try pulling and releasing, pummelling, hacking and nipping. Push the soft flesh up towards the back and outwards – stretching movements that stimulate the genital area without actually touching it.

LEGS AND ARMS

One of the great benefits of erotic massage is the feeling it gives of being cherished all over. Yet some parts of the body get badly neglected – how often do you touch or caress your partner's lower legs or feet? Study her limbs in detail as you stroke them to learn their contours and feel the flesh and muscles respond under your touch – it will give your partner a blissful feeling of security and belonging.

SEXUAL TENSION BUSTER 2

Get the circulation going and the blood oxygenated by working the legs and arms towards the heart.

1 With your partner lying on her back, start at the ankles. Wrap your hands around them, making close contact with your palms and fingers against her skin. With all circulation strokes, the idea is to move the hands together, pushing the blood in the direction of the heart. Work up the legs, and as you come back down again, keep the pressure in the same direction, towards the heart.

2 Now work the arms in the same way, again with the strokes in the direction of the heart.

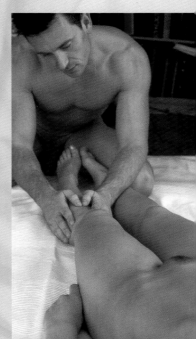

WHILE YOU'RE THERE

With your partner lying on her back, raise her lower leg to make a right angle with the floor. Lean forwards and rest the sole of her foot on your chest. Wrap your hands round the calf and massage it deeply towards the heart, applying little circles of pressure with your thumbs.

Massage your partner's inner thighs with deep thumb pressure. Work up to the genitals but don't touch them. An invigorating massage will get the blood pumping in the genital area.

23

FOCUS ON THE KNEE

Next it's the turn of the knees, another erotically sensitive but neglected part of the body. The knee is the body's most complicated joint. After releasing tension in the muscles around it, you can turn your attention to the knee itself and massage easch one in turn.

SEXUAL TENSION BUSTER 3

1 With him lying on his back, work on the fronts of his legs from ankle to thigh. Glide your hands up and down the outsides of his legs.

2 Knead with gentle pressure either side of the shin. Work vigorously on the thighs, kneading until his flesh feels warm and tingling with life.

3 Sitting alongside the lower leg, raise his knee slightly from the floor, taking its weight in both hands. With your fingers under the knee and your thumbs above it, brush your thumbs repeatedly over the kneecap with the lightest of strokes.

4 Work your thumbs very gently in the groove below the kneecap, while stroking your fingers in and around the crease at the back of the knee. Avoid pressing against the tendons. As you build up speed you and your partner will feel a pleasant relaxing warmth gathering in the area.

WHILE YOU'RE THERE

Position yourself just below your partner's hips. Raise the leg nearest you, supporting it with one hand clasping the calf and the other under the thigh. Then, still holding the calf, place the palm of your other hand on the front of his leg just below his knee and push forwards with your body weight, so that his leg bends at the knee, his knee moves towards his chest, and his heel touches his thigh.

Stop as soon as you feel resistance – don't force the leg, as this could be painful.

Repeat, stretching the leg out and folding it towards his body five times. You should feel him relax a little more each time.

Do the same with the other leg. This exercise is very expansive and gives a great sensation of freedom and openness. Use this move to indirectly stimulate and improve blood supply to the genital area.

UP AND DOWN TO THE FEET

Worries about sex cause tension to build up in the legs. Sometimes this leads to cramps in the calf muscles, which tend to strike during the small hours of the night. Practise this move as part of your erotic massage to keep the legs relaxed and supple.

SEXUAL TENSION BUSTER 4

Compression using your forearm makes warm pleasant feelings travel up and down your partner's leg. Oil your forearm to make it glide more smoothly across her leg – the more hair on your arms, the more oil you will need to use.

1 Lift your partner's leg with both hands and hold the ankle to raise the knee comfortably. Clench your fist to tighten the muscles in your arm, then press the inside of your forearm against her calf, just above the ankle. Pulling towards your body, move your arm up towards her knee, rotating it as if you were polishing her leg.

2 From the knee, lean forwards and work on the upper side of her thigh, bearing down with your weight and continuing to 'polish' her thigh.

3 Repeat several times then lower her leg gently. Repeat on the other leg.

WHILE YOU'RE THERE

Try this with the feet. Sit facing the tops of her feet with your back towards her face. Hold one foot in both hands and work delicately with your thumbs, feeling around all the bones of the feet from the base of the toes up towards the ankle. Do not spoil the mood by tickling your partner with a feathery touch on her soles.

Move to below her feet. Hold the foot up, support it under the calf or ankle and press deeply on the sole with your thumb or the heel of the other hand, working round the contours of the foot. Lower the foot and work on the toes. Work delicately on each toe, moving with small twiddlings of finger and thumb that feel all the tiny bones from the base to the tip. Then pull off at the tip, as if you were pulling off socks with toes in them.

27

BELLY AND CHEST

Massaging the torso helps to free the rib cage from tension, making it easier to breathe deeply and relax. Place your palms on your partner's belly and ask her to breathe from here, so you can feel it rise and fall. Shallow breaths from the chest don't use the lungs fully, so stale air is never properly expelled and the blood doesn't get its maximum dose of oxygen.

SEXUAL TENSION BUSTER 5

1 With your partner lying on her back, start with broad gliding strokes over the whole torso. Don't forget that you are treating all body parts equally, so avoid the temptation to pay special attention to her breasts – in fact it's much more exciting for her that your hands will slide over and around them – it heightens anticipation for later.

2 Using two hands, palms down, glide across the abdomen. Start with one hand under the breastbone and the other just above the pubic hair and move them in clockwise circles, with the

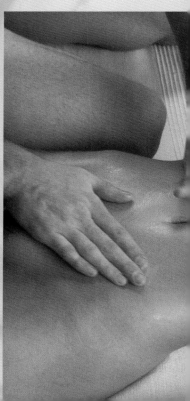

lower hand brushing across the upper hand where they meet at the navel. It is important that you use a clockwise motion because this follows the movements of the bowel.

3 Next try a merry-go-round movement – while one palm describes a broad circle around the navel, use the fingers of the other hand to sketch a detailed spiral scribble along its path.

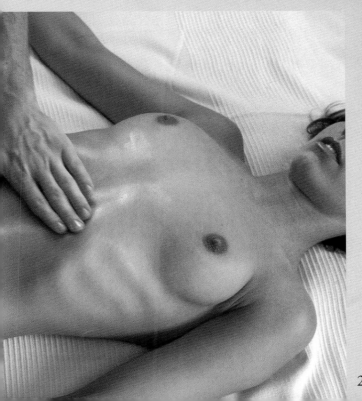

4 Move to your partner's side to work the rib cage. Lean over to the opposite side of her body, cup your hands over her side and drag them alternately towards you, feeling with your fingers between her ribs and wriggling them loose. Apply firm pressure to avoid tickling. Work right down the side of the body, going over and over your tracks. Keep up these movements in a steady rhythm and it will feel to her as though lots of hands are touching her at once.

LIFT AND FLOAT

This movement floods the head with oxygenated blood to revive the brain – superb for relieving headaches. To be picked up and held like this is an emotive experience.

SEXUAL TENSION BUSTER 6

1 If your right leg is the stronger, kneel to her left; if your left leg is stronger, kneel to her right. Interlace your fingers and clasp your hands beneath her waist. Tell her to keep her body limp. Put your stronger foot forwards and raise yourself off the ground, lifting your partner's waist at your hips and bearing her weight on your leg.
2 Hold her in this position for 20 seconds or more, then lower her, supporting her neck if you can.
3 Without losing contact, repeat the motion several times. As soon as after the first lift, you should notice a difference. Her face will be slightly flushed, her eyes shining, and small tension lines will have disappeared.

> **Caution** Don't try to lift a partner who is heavier than you. Watch out for her neck as you lower her. Start with her neck at the edge of the bed so that her head slides back as you lie her down.

WHILE YOU'RE THERE

Finish with an all-over body stroke.

Oil your palms. Cup her legs just above her ankles with your fingers. Push firmly and smoothly up the legs and over the torso with your fingertips. Let your hands part under her neck and move outwards over her shoulders.

Sweep your hands round her shoulders and back to her torso again just below the armpits. Run your hands down her sides to the ankles. Repeat several times.

FACE AND HEAD

The daily pleasure of rubbing cleansers and moisturizers into the skin, and an occasional facial or relaxing scalp massage at the hairdresser's are treats most men miss. An erotic face and head massage is one such treat. You won't need oil.

SEXUAL TENSION BUSTER 7

Let a combination of your intuition and your partner's responses guide you as you sit behind his head and try the following movements:

1 Starting with your fingers under his chin, sweep the flats of your hands up the sides of his face, pulling the flesh taut at the temples and following through by running your fingers through his hair.

2 Work in tiny circles just below the jawbone, starting at the tip of the chin and moving right round to just under the ears.

3 Join the tips of your index fingers under his nose and the tips of your middle fingers below his mouth. Pull your fingers towards the corners of his mouth, drawing a smile around it. Let them follow under the cheekbones, up the sides of his face and over his ears.

4 Slide your fingers under the ears and work them firmly along the groove between the ear and the face. Wiggle and swirl the fingertips inside the ear flaps. Gently twiddle the earlobes between your fingers and thumbs.

5 Working from the base of the neck, raise his head in both hands, stretch his neck, then rake with your fingertips through his hair as you let his head relax gently back on the pillow. At first he will probably keep his neck held stiff – tell him that you need to feel the weight of his head in your hands. This is a wonderful movement to relieve neck pain.

6 With your two index fingers, make small circling movements on the face at either side of the nostrils. Work up the sides of the nose then work the bridge, but take care to avoid the delicate skin around the eyes.

7 Cup the sides of the forehead in your hands and work with small circling movements from the bridge of the nose along the eyebrows, stretching them as you go. Very delicately smooth the skin under the brows with your fingertips in outward sweeping stokes.

8 Starting from the bridge of the nose, pass alternate hands lightly across the brow and into the hair.

9 Give the scalp an invigorating massage, whirling your thumbs and fingertips all over it, softly tugging his hair if he likes it. Finish by holding the top of his head in your hands.

WHILE YOU'RE THERE

Give him a relaxing scalp massage hairdresser-style. Seat him comfortably where you can wet his hair with a shower attachment, and lovingly shampoo his hair. Make sure that the water is the right temperature for him, and take time over each step, using the lather to massage every inch of scalp. Rinse well, sweeping and squeezing his hair with your hands.

PRESSURE BOOST

Try a regular massage of specific pressure points to boost your sexual energy. The Japanese therapy of shiatsu is based on the philosophy and medical theory of acupuncture. It means 'finger pressure', but therapists also use the palms of their hands and sometimes elbows, knees and feet to apply stronger pressure. Shiatsu works with the flow of energy called ki that runs through the body in channels known as meridians. By working pressure points along these meridians, blockages can be dissolved and the flow of energy released.

THE KIDNEY MERIDIAN

It takes years to train as a professional shiatsu practitioner, but there are some pressure points that you can experiment with on your partner at home – work them to increase and strengthen the flow of their sexual energy.

Sexuality is governed, for the most part, by the kidney meridian. The kidney pressure points, or *tsubos*, are found about one thumb's width, or *cun*, on either side of the spine, level with the

your tongue right up the centre of the chest, then zigzag across the lines of the ribs in and out to the sides. Circle the breasts and flick and suck the nipples.

HOT MASSAGE IDEAS

- Massage with the vulva: straddle your partner and massage his oiled torso with your vulva.
- Hair massage: you can do this even if you have fairly short hair – but don't oil his body first. Lean over his torso and brush your hair up and down and round and round.
- Nipple massage: lean over him and massage him with your nipples, in broad strokes up and down his body, or gyrating and drawing circles on his skin. Massage his penis between your breasts.
- Foot massage: dangle your legs above your partner and trace patterns on his oiled body with your big toes.

rippling motion, then work on the buttocks, pushing them up and apart. Tug at the flesh with your lips. Nuzzle the inner thighs and tickle them with your tongue.

Then probe the navel with your tongue and lap like a cat clockwise round the belly. Draw a firm wavy line with

Set the scene

To heighten expectation, your awareness of each other and the fulfilment that lies ahead, investigate the power of fragrance to relax, stimulate and reawaken your erotic memories. If it excites you, explore the possibility of body piercing. Titillate with sexy underwear, and have fun together performing provocative belly dances.

FRAGRANCE

The sense of smell is strongly connected to memory and emotion. The right smell provides a relaxing background to lovemaking. Try fresh flowers, baking bread or cakes, ripe peaches and apricots, furniture polish or clean sheets. Lavender, pumpkin pie, cinnamon, liquorice and doughnuts have been found to induce stronger erections in American men – warm, homely smells that make them feel happy and secure.

THE SCENT OF LOVE

The natural perfume of a clean woman is called her *cassolette* – French for perfume box. Inhale it from her hair, skin, armpits, genitals and the clothes she has been wearing. The natural smell of both sexes forms a strong part in sexual attraction – marriage counsellors know that an aversion to a partner's smell is one thing no amount of therapy can overturn.

Use your lover's smell to excite you – bury your head in an old T-shirt before you meet. Or use it to calm and

comfort you after a row. The smell will remind you of why you are together.

ROSE PETALS

Buy her roses, or pick them from the garden. Then drop the petals one by one on her naked body. Sniff their fragrance – lick round them lovingly and press them into her skin with your tongue. Finally, make love with the petals crushed between you.

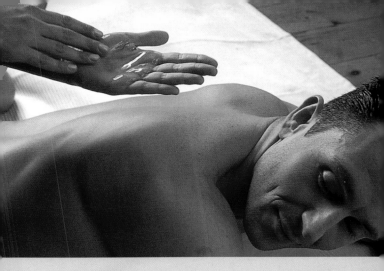

AROMATHERAPY OILS FOR EROTIC MASSAGE

- Frankincense: a spicy woody aroma known for its aphrodisiac properties. It relaxes, rejuvenates and enlivens the emotions
- Geranium: a floral scent that has a relieving effect on anxiety
- Jasmine: rich, exotic and sensual, this lifts the mood and is highly regarded for its aphrodisiac effect
- Juniper: a woody scent that is good for stimulating and relaxing. Relieves stress and fatigue
- Patchouli: a seductive Oriental aroma and the base of many heavy perfumes. Redolent of the harem
- Ylang ylang: an exotic, Far-Eastern scent that is used as a love potion. Very effective both as a stimulant and a sedative

BODY PIERCING

Erotic piercing has been popular in many cultures for centuries. Rings and jewels can be worn anywhere that can be pierced – not only the ears, nose and eyebrows, but also through the tongue, nipples, navel, penis, scrotum and labia. Some couples wear gold rings in their genitals instead of wedding rings.

EROTIC RINGS

Rings in the labia don't increase erotic sensation – they are worn simply for their looks. Sometimes rings on either side of the vulva are used to pull back the labia for sex.

According to Arab tradition, rings in the scrotum prevent the testicles from ever rising back into the body.

In the South Pacific, a ring called a *guiche* is placed at the point where the scrotum joins the perineum, in front of the anus. If correctly placed, it is

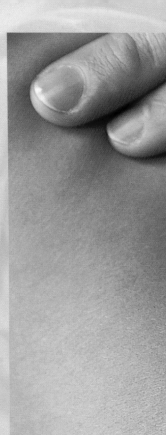

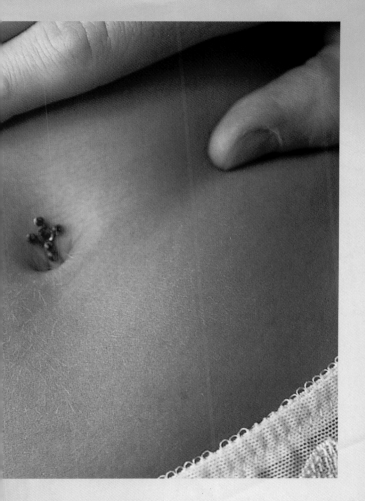

51

said to intensify and prolong orgasms when gently pulled.

The Southeast Asian *ampallang* is a rod that pierces horizontally through the glans of the penis above the urethra. It is said to increase firmness during erection. Sometimes the rod has a ring around it that encircles the glans. Bead-like protuberances on the ring are designed to stimulate the vulva and clitoris during sex.

Queen Victoria's consort Prince Albert is attributed with the invention of the penis ring named after him, though he is said to have tied a cord through it to his leg to stop involuntary nocturnal erections.

Nipple rings were worn by Roman centurions, who used them as fixings for their cloaks. Victorian women also wore them to simulate their nipples under their clothes.

Caution Piercing can be dangerous. Not only is it painful at the time, the pain may last months while the wound heals and infection can easily set in. Many people are allergic to the metals used in piercing needles or in jewellery. Some piercings may result in permanent nerve damage.

Always choose a licensed practitioner, preferably one who has been personally recommended to you. Wash the wound daily with a recommended antiseptic, rotating the ring or bar to keep the hole open, until it has healed.

LINGERIE

Beautiful underwear boosts a woman's self-confidence – and a man's morale – only he will get to know what she wears under her clothes when they're out together: a filmy teddy, a lacy bustier, or just stockings and suspenders. Lingerie makes a woman feel pampered and luxurious. It fits in the same seductive part of the imagination as high heels and make-up, and in the bedroom it allows her to play the vamp.

THE BUYER'S GUIDE

Men who buy women sexy underwear are sometimes accused of buying themselves a present – put this right by taking your partner along to choose the gift herself. She's the expert on fit, style and the colour to suit her skin, she knows whether she wants lace or leopard. Most importantly, she knows what makes her feel sexy – and if it's magic for her it will work for you too. And in the shop you'll get to see her model a whole selection of gorgeous lingerie.

A GUIDE FOR THE UNINITIATED

A woman can use lingerie to send a signal her partner won't miss – dressing for bed in a cosy nightie and a pair of

woolly socks means she needs a good night's sleep, but appearing in a black lace bustier means something else...

- A teddy is an all-in-one with a fitted bra top – go for filmy, lacy fabric.
- A camisole is a fitted top that sometimes incorporates a bra. They come in soft cotton knits

or fresh crisp broderie anglaise, which is a cotton fabric decorated with little embroidered holes.

- The craze for corsets has revived with the bustier, a sexy sculptured one-piece garment that incorporates an uplift-bra, nips in at the waist and hugs her figure as far as the hips. This very

dressy item comes in luxury fabrics and finishes and luscious colours. The right fit will do wonders for almost every figure – so make this your choice for a special gift, but let her try it first.

- A suspender belt and stockings is a good gift to buy as a surprise – you'll need to know her waist and hip size.

- Something else you can safely buy her if you know her size is a selection of silk bikini thongs. At the front is the merest scrap of colour and at the back, a thong that disappears between her buttocks. A thong is great for emphasizing a curvaceous behind and as a bonus is invisible under even the thinnest pair of trousers.

SEX GOD

Does your lover have a secret longing to be a glamorous rock-star? Would you like to play groupie to an androgynous god? Exploring the characteristics of the opposite sex within ourselves is an intriguing part of understanding the human psyche. To break down the boundaries of sexism – and treat yourself to a powerful erotic turn-on – vamp up your man to give him a mysteriously ambivalent new sexuality.

TURNING THE TABLES

Women can express their feelings about power and domination by wearing masculine clothes any day of the week, but it's a different matter for men – Western dress codes deny them a whole world of colour and sensuousness. So lock the door, get out the make-up and get imaginative. Act out your fantasy. Think of Queen Zinua of Angola. In the 17th century she kept a collection of husbands permanently dressed as women.

PAMPER YOUR PARTNER

Relax him first with a proper beauty session. Give him a luxurious bath and shampoo with scalp massage followed by an all-over body rub with aromatherapy oils and a facial. Put cucumber slices on his eyelids, play music, work magic on his skin with dreamy fingers.

Apply just a touch of make-up – darken his lashes with mascara and add mystery to his eyes with kohl. Subtly redden his lips. Manicure and buff his nails or add pearly varnish that tones with his skin. Turn him into a film star.

Now experiment with clothes – think drama, glamour, beauty – and create an appearance that you both love to look at. Try torn Tshirts, jewels or a studded leather collar. Or experience the thrilling contrast of delicate silk against a rough male skin, as you attire your man in an exotic Eastern sarong.

The perfect way to end this particular game is for the newly created sex god to act out any fantasy he desires. Let him take charge and make love to him in whatever way he wants you to.

BELLY DANCING

In the East, a woman's gently rounded belly is one of her most sensual features, appreciated to the full in the skilful, sensuous art of belly dancing. The undulating hips suggest burning passion.

THE BELLY ROLL

One of the key movements of belly dancing, this relaxes and sensitizes the whole body, and gives sexual confidence. Place your thumbs on your navel with your palms flat on your lower belly. Push the lower belly out, then pull it in and up as far as you can. Push your diaphragm out and let your belly roll down and out. Begin slowly, repeat and speed up to a steady rhythm.

The belly flutter works on the diaphragm. Hold your breath or open your mouth and pant. Pull the diaphragm, in then push it out. Repeat slowly at first, then speed up until your belly is vibrating.

THE HIP ROLL

Stand relaxed and upright, with your arms out to the sides, palms facing up. Push the right hip out to the side. Push the pelvis forward as far as you can and roll your hips over to the left. Push the pelvis back to the rear, sticking your bottom out. Straighten up, then roll the hips to the right. Roll the hips in a smooth circle, as if you were using a hula hoop.

THE BENEFITS

An awareness of the belly as the centre of the self gives confidence and solidity, it improves the posture, eases stress and lifts depression, as well as exercising and toning many of the muscles used in sex. Above all, it gives you a sense of vitality and a belief in your own erotic power. Try the exercises, then make up variations. Add some silk scarves and jewels, dramatize your eyes with kohl and prepare to amaze your lover.

61

Titillation

To get the most fun possible out of sex, explore your own and your partner's responses in great detail so you can learn to play each other's bodies like a musical instrument. Add spice to your love life by acting out your fantasies. Discover the secret of keeping your sex life alive with imagination and variety.

APHRODISIACS

The body's most important sex organ is the brain – and when it comes to aphrodisiacs you can be sure it's almost always in the mind. Canadian researchers recently tested the drug yohimbine, extracted from the yohimbe plant, which is used by the Bantu people of Africa as a male aphrodisiac. They found that 42 per cent of a group of men with erection difficulties responded well to the treatment – but so did 28 per cent of the control group, who were all given sugar pill placebos.

SEX AND DRUGS

Everyone knows that alcohol loosens the tongue and the inhibitions – but though it enlivens at first, it's basically a depressant. A little too much and you'll be drowsy – more than that and the urge and ability will leave altogether. It

is preferable to go for quality not quantity – share one good bottle of wine with an excellent meal and intimate conversation to put you in the mood for love.

One survey conducted in Italy found that while men reported increased sexual satisfaction with Viagra, their partners were not impressed. If you try Viagra don't forget to make your partner feel that you want her – not just your own satisfaction.

Recreational drugs, like alcohol, induce a chemical high followed by an emotional low, while dreamy cannabis encourages sleep, rather than great sex. Ask yourselves whether it's sex you want, or each other. It can be a lonely and alienating experience if you get the feeling your partner's deriving their pleasure from taking a drug instead of just from being with you.

If you smoke, you should be aware that nicotine reduces

the production of nitric oxide, which is the body's main chemical messenger that triggers the pumping of blood to the penis.

THE POWER OF THOUGHT

Whether it's oysters, caviar or wild yams, if you like it, believe in it and are in the right mood for it to work, then work it surely will. Give thanks for the positive power of thought. Something that often does the trick is dark chocolate. It stimulates the brain to produce phenylethylamine, a chemical that is triggered when we fall in love. So putting a chocolate on your lover's pillow really will send a sexy message... Try sharing a chocolate kiss. You can even buy chocolate-flavoured body paint, so why wait until you get to heaven...

BEDTIME STORIES

In your imagination, set the scene for an erotic encounter. Describe it to your partner and then ask him or her to tell you what happens next. Interrupt the flow of the story only to ask for more specific details.

SCENE SETTERS
The following are suggested scenes for you to try. You could also take scenes from your favourite books or films and continue them in whatever way your imaginations suggest.

1 In a private room in a Turkish bath, a young man lies naked on his belly, his eyes closed, beads of sweat trickling down his hot, damp skin as he waits for his massage. Strong hands begin to work on his back: they knead and pull at his buttocks, spreading the flesh and teasing the root of his balls. He groans and parts his legs; a hand slips between them, clasping and rocking his balls as his penis becomes erect…

2 Peach Blossom leads her friend Little Star to her boudoir. They love to spend hours together dressing up, wrapping each other in lengths of fine silk, while they are planning for Peach Blossom's forthcoming wedding day. 'No, wear it like this!' says Little Star. She smoothes the silky material across Peach Blossom's naked

69

breasts. The two girls gaze
deeply into one another's eyes
as her fingers caress her
friend's taut nipples, then
their breath mingles and their
lips meet…

3 A carriage with its blinds
drawn pulls into a courtyard,
the door is opened from
inside and the eagerly waiting
Lady Emmeline steps aboard.
'Drive on to the Bois de

Boulogne!' says the prince. The driver understands. The Bois is a favourite venue for illicit lovers – the horses will walk slowly, the gentle rocking motion of the carriage adding to the lovers' secret pleasure. Emmeline sighs and lies back among the soft velvet cushions as their hands and eyes find each other in the gloom…

SEX TALK

Intimate sounds – sighs and groans of satisfaction – are a terrific turn-on. And for some people it is sex talk that drives them really wild. Men and women both love to hear their partners verbally let rip – some relish it all, from whispered endearments to crude commentary and obscenities.

WHY FILTHY TALK IS A TURN-ON

Simply, because it's forbidden – so the more unusual it is for your partner to use four-letter words and language that makes the air go blue, the more exciting it's likely to be for you. To express what usually takes place only inside your head is to break down yet another inhibition and release more

pent-up libido you didn't know you had.

The sad thing about obscenities in many languages is that we use forbidden sex words to express anger and as insults. In less-repressed cultures, sex words are used only for sex. So a Swede might shout something about yellow snow and a Native American might call someone a failed horse-breaker, but neither would use 'fuck' except to express pleasure. Try using words as they were originally intended and feel their erotic power.

SAY IT TO ME

During long slow thrusting a man can whisper his secret lusts and desires for her into his partner's ear. He can tell her what he's planning to do to her next, then do it.

Tell your partner what feels good and how wonderful it feels while he's actually doing it, and it will rouse his passion even more. It's a fantastic ego-boost that can spur your lover on to more imaginative and longer-lasting sex.

Tell your partner your fantasies during mutual masturbation – especially erotic daydreams that feature him or her having sex with someone else. This is a very good way to work yourselves up into a very steamy lather.

Telephone sex can be a real turn-on. When you and your lover are apart and long for sex, let the telephone bring you together. Detailed descriptions of what you are both doing and feeling are the next best things to being there in person.

Je t'aime. Lots of people like to be talked to in bed in a foreign language – whether they understand it or not.

BLINDFOLD SENSATIONS

Blindfold your lover to heighten her sense of touch, then try different sensations – texture, temperature, pressure – on various parts of her body. Keep it slow and full of surprises. Find out which parts are most sensitive to each mystery stimulant – get her to guess what's happening to her.

STIMULATING SENSATIONS

- Cool treat: ice cream and fruit sorbets are edible coolants to use imaginatively and deliciously on your partner's body.
- Ice: cool your partner down with ice during a sexual massage. The forehead is an obvious place to start, or doodle around the nipples with an ice cube, then circle

tantalizingly around the belly, over the inner thighs and across the genitals. (Never use dry ice, as it will stick to and burn the skin.)

- More ice: try giving your partner oral sex with crushed ice in your mouth. During fellatio this technique is sometimes used to delay orgasm.
- Hot air: heat up your mouth with a warm drink before you go down on your partner.

- Hot compress: fit an inflatable bath pillow filled with hot water under her neck and place miniature hot water bottles at strategic points on her body. Or use little 'beanbags' of wheat heated up in the microwave. Now doodle round the beanbags with a feather, an ice cube or warm spoons that have been dipped in oil.
- Fur: let the animal inside her loose by stroking her

skin with fur, real or fake –
it feels especially lovely on
the chest and belly.

- Rhythm: use the tasselled
drumsticks from a snare
drum to whip up a rhythm
on her back or buttocks, or
try an egg whisk made of
pliant twigs, or even the
tassels on curtain tie-backs.

- Feathers: try stroking your
lover's skin with a feather
or a swansdown boa.

- Marbles: massage his chest
and stomach with a handful
of marbles, rolling them in
small clockwise circles.

- Rice and confetti: shower
him with rice, or pour it in
a stream all down his spine.
Drift confetti on to his
cheeks, neck and genitals.

- Sweet sensation: dribble
warm honey on to his erect
penis and suck it off.

- Gel: rub squidgy gel into
nipples and genitals. Pay
thorough attention to the
inner thighs and perineum
before you move on to
scrotum and penis.

Explore

Study the sensitivity of your partner's main erogenous zones in minute detail, to familiarize yourself with their special desires and needs. Experiment with different types of friction with your tongue, fingers and genitals to discover the best way to arouse them. Then investigate ways of varying stimulation so that you can pace arousal. Control of timing is the secret of long-lasting, satisfying sex.

KISSING

Kissing is the greatest turn-on there is, because it shows your partner what an expert lover you are. New couples put all their erotic feelings into kissing. A deep French kiss in a passionate clinch is one sure sign that bed is on the agenda.

SO WHAT MAKES A GREAT KISSER?

Be imaginative with your lips and tongue. Use their mobility and suppleness to communicate your feelings.

Probe with your tongue in your partner's mouth, but don't dart it in and out like a lizard or shove it aggressively down the throat. Try gently sucking on your partner's tongue or lower lip.

Who takes the lead? Try leading yourself or tune into your partner's kiss. Or play passive and allow yourself to be kissed – this can feel particularly good for a man

who feels he's usually expected to be dominant.

Pay attention to the corners of your partner's mouth with your tongue, pushing it inside the mouth to echo the feeling of the penis pushing inside the vagina.

Have your partner open their mouth and bare the tongue, then lick across it with generous broad strokes from corner to corner – an especially arousing kiss.

In a prolonged kissing session the shorter partner often gets a crick in the neck, so try kissing on the stairs or use a footstool.

What to do with your hands? Cradle your partner's face, support their neck, stroke their hair. Some people are driven wild by a finger gently inserted into their mouth along with your tongue.

Kiss other parts of the body, not just the mouth. Many women love having their palms, wrists, foreheads and eyelids gently kissed.

83

SECRET EROGENOUS ZONES

*Giving your lover detailed
attention is a powerful
turn-on – you might be the
first person to explore places
like the crook of the arm,
behind the knee or the nape
of the neck since your lover
was a small child.*

THE EAR
There's a theory that people
with similar earlobes are
unconsciously attracted to
each other. How do yours
match up? Some people love
having their earlobes nibbled
and sucked. A few even adore

to have their ears licked, with the tongue slowly swirling round the contours of the ear flap and flicking down inside. Ask first, in case your lover finds it ticklish or a turn-off.

THE FEET

Try sucking your partner's toes one by one. Experiment with using the man's big toe as a penis substitute – some women find this very erotic. Short nails and smooth skin, please. It adds a new dimension to games of footsie under the table. A foot bath in scented hot water for tired feet is a lovely treat when one of you comes in exhausted.

THE NAVEL

Lick with the flat of your tongue in broad stokes, sweeping in a clockwise direction around the navel and circling inwards. Then hold your partner's buttocks with one hand, pressing the heel of the hand very firmly into the perineum and pulling upwards, and dance the tip of your tongue all around and over the belly button, exploring every tiny crevice. Hit the right nerve here and you'll send a tingling sensation streaking right down to the genitals.

THE BUTTOCKS

There's lots of scope on this fleshy part for vigorous activity, such as kneading, playful smacks, sucking and nibbling – but don't neglect the sensitivity of the skin.

Stroke the buttocks ever so lightly with your palm and fingertips, trailing your hand in lazy circles around their curves. Note that the buttocks make a wonderful pillow for relaxing after lovemaking.

87

HAIR

The hair has always held sexual magic. Lovers once exchanged locks. In some cultures the bride and groom are shampooed together at their wedding, then their hair is twisted together to unite them. Hair symbolised sexual energy for men; cutting it meant castration.

FOLLOW THE *KAMA SUTRA*

Students of the *Kama Sutra* learned the arts of beautifying head hair with henna and dressing it in braids and topknots of flowers. While the hair on the head was celebrated, men shaved their beards and both sexes removed body hair.

ANCIENT INDIAN INSPIRATION

1 One of the best ways to kindle hot desire in a woman is at the time of rising, softly to hold and handle her hair...

2 The man encloses her hair between his two palms behind her head, at the same time kissing her lower lip...

3 'The dragon's turn' is when the standing man, much excited by the approaching prospect of sexual congress, amorously seizes the hind knot of the woman's hair, at the same time as he closely embraces her.

4 'Holding the crest-hair of love' is when, during the act of copulation, the man holds his partner's hair above her ears, while she does the same to him, and both exchange frequent kisses.

TRY THIS

Dress your hair for love with a daisy chain or a garland of ivy or vine leaves.

Sex without pubic hair feels closer still – more naked, more vulnerable. So make a ritual of shaping your pubic hair or removing it entirely. If shaving irritates, use a depilatory cream.

THE BREASTS

Observe your partner's breasts during sex. Women react in different ways: many develop a flush that spreads from above the waist right across their chest. The areola – the dark disc around the nipple – may swell or get darker. In many women the nipples become erect, for some during foreplay, and for some more strongly or earlier in one breast than the other. A woman's breasts can swell as much as 25 per cent when she is aroused.

SENSITIVITY

The upper breast is generally more sensitive than the lower breast. This discovery was made by scientists at Vienna University, who tested 150 women by blindfolding them and pricking their breasts with pins. Amazingly, they found that the nipple was the least sensitive part.

They also discovered that large breasts are 24 per cent less sensitive than smaller breasts – because the nerve that transmits sensation from the nipple is stretched.

Sagging breasts are least sensitive because nerves are stretched and compressed by the weight of the breasts. Consequently, she will feel better lying on her back. Push her breasts gently upwards as you fondle them. Try gentle kneading and experimental nibbling.

BREAST AWARENESS

Remember that breasts can be very tender around the time of a woman's period.

Cup and lift the breasts in both hands, massaging underneath them with a gentle circular motion.

Large areolas have more nerve endings, so don't stimulate nipples or areolas until she is fully aroused. Instead caress the outsides of the breasts.

Small areolas have fewer nerve endings and are less responsive. Work in tantalizing swirls with your tongue around the nipple, focusing on the areola and the sensitive skin in the upper third of the breast.

Small breasts can be massaged in an all-over chest massage with the palms of the hands. Be tender but firm, not tentative.

If she's had a successful breast implant, sensitivity won't be impaired, but take care in moving her breasts. Avoid vigorous handling and use feathery caresses with fingers or tongue.

Breastfeeding makes nipples tender. Leave them for the baby. Lightly stroke swollen breasts on the less sensitive underside.

THE VAGINA

Explore your partner's vagina as if you had never seen or felt a vagina before. Kneel on the floor with your partner lying with her bottom on the edge of the bed. Make yourself comfortable between her legs and begin by gently stroking the flats of your palms across her pubic hair and upper thighs. Gently part her legs and put her feet on your shoulders before you venture further.

EXPLORING THE VAGINA

Stroke the whole area, just very lightly, then press your open lips to the skin of her upper thigh and breathe warm air on to it, circling the vulva and eventually homing in on it. Don't use your tongue. She will now be feeling warm, relaxed and very responsive. Part the pubic hair and very gently explore the shape of her vulva with your fingers.

93

Delicately open the outer lips and this time breathe (not blow) warm air on to the open vulva without touching it with your lips.

INSIDE THE VULVA

Begin to explore the vulva with your fingers, moving very slowly and lightly from the outside inwards. Don't touch her clitoris yet. Read her responses carefully and let them dictate your movement. Gradually build up rhythm and speed as if you were playing a living musical instrument. Use light flicking or rubbing movements, all the while using less pressure than you think she might be ready for so that her body movements continually beg you for more.

When you are sure the juices are flowing, dip your

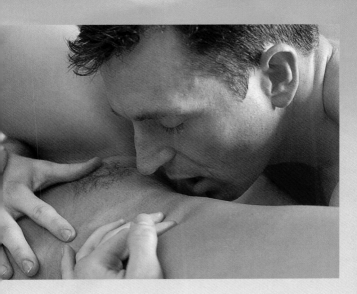

finger briefly into her vagina. Begin to explore it by darting in and out and let her thrust against you rather than press your fingers all the way in yourself. Keep withdrawing and playing the vulva with your fingertips.

Once you are deep inside her vagina, learn its shape, snugness and angle within her body. The better you know it, the more pleasure you can give her during intercourse, and the less chance you will have of hurting her by stabbing at the wrong angle. Right at the top of the vagina is something that feels a bit like the cap of a mushroom. This is the cervix, the neck of the womb.

Caution: Never blow into the vagina – it could cause serious harm.

THE G-SPOT

Controversy surrounds the mysterious G-spot – a sensitive area half way up the front wall of the vagina. Ernst Grafenberg, who discovered it, claimed that when it was stimulated, a woman would have an orgasm accompanied by an ejaculation of sexual fluid similar in composition to the secretions of the male prostate.

DOES THE G-SPOT REALLY EXIST?

In one US survey, 40 per cent of women claim to ejaculate in this way, but another survey shows fewer than 5 per cent believe that it has happened to them. Conduct your own experiments with your fingers or concentrate on sex positions that target the spot.

IF SO, WHERE?

Grafenberg, working in the 1940s, advised that the newly discovered erotic hot spot

swelled when stimulated with firm, deep, continuous pressure, becoming a tiny female erection. The best way to do this is for the woman to lie on the bed on her front, legs slightly apart and buttocks slightly raised. Insert two fingers into her vagina, palm down, and explore the front wall of the vagina. Ask her to tell you what feels good. She may have a brief sensation that she's about to urinate, which gives way to erotic pleasure. If there is any ejaculate, take a good look at it. Some say it is colourless, some say it is milky like semen. Still others believe that due to loss of pelvic muscle control, some women squirt urine as they come.

and warmth pools out through the rest of her body. A woman's body also produces an ejaculation, which happens at the same time inside the womb, which has become drenched with wetness, as well as on the outside, because the vagina is now gaping and open.'

TRYING IT OUT

Experiment with stimulating the G-spot during intercourse. Try it with the woman lying on her front and the man entering from behind, or the woman lying on her back with a bolster cushion under her buttocks to raise them for easier access, or on all-fours, doggy style. If the man lies down and the woman sits astride him facing his feet, she can control the angle of penetration herself. If you prove the existence of the G-spot, great – if you prove it doesn't exist, you will at least have had a lot of fun trying to locate it.

ANCIENT WISDOM

The idea that women can also ejaculate dates back to the ancient Greeks and possibly even earlier. Here's what Hippocrates wrote in 400BC: 'During intercourse, when a woman's genitals are vigorously rubbed and her womb titillated, lustfulness overwhelms her down below, and the feeling of pleasure

The hands-on approach

Remember the days when intercourse was strictly off-limits, and sexual satisfaction depended on the inventiveness that resulted? Heavy petting and mutual masturbation can open a world of pleasure for both partners. Having your partner do the work to bring you to climax is an intensely pleasing experience. Repaying the compliment is similarly satisfying.

HEAVY PETTING

Get imaginative and invent new ways of having sex without intercourse to rediscover the steamy days of your youth. Heavy petting stops short of genital-to-genital contact (originally as a contraceptive measure or to keep her virginity intact) – but anything else goes, creating an almost unbearably heady mix of frustration and excitement.

SEX WITHOUT INTERCOURSE

If you don't like menstrual blood, but she feels particularly raunchy when she has a period, sex without intercourse could be one solution. It's also a great way to go if your sex life has grown tired or predictable and has become just a one-track route to orgasm. There's certainly no pressure to perform if intercourse is off the menu.

KEEP YOUR CLOTHES ON

Start fully clothed, then just loosen or remove clothing as required, but agree in advance that she will keep her panties on and there won't be any penetration. Move through a variety of sex positions (this is a good way to practice new moves for the real thing on another occasion). The friction of his penis against her vulva might well give her an orgasm, but don't carry on so long that it makes him sore.

BETWEEN THE BREASTS

Many men fantasize about coming between a woman's breasts. Best done with him sitting in a chair with legs splayed, and his lover kneeling in front of him. She begins by caressing his penis with her breasts and tickling the glans with her nipples, then squeezes him between her breasts and works up and down, holding the base of the penis with one

103

hand and pressing her breasts together with the other. Add oil and work with passion. A smaller woman can try masturbating him against her breasts while caressing them with her other hand.

BETWEEN THE THIGHS
The woman clenches her partner's penis between her thighs at the very top – in either the missionary position or with her lying on her back

or crouching on all-fours. If he ejaculates, it's very easy for sperm to get transferred to the vagina, so note this is not a good position to try if contraception is vital.

MUTUAL MASTURBATION
This is a delicious way of satisfying each other, whether it's during heavy petting or only a part of a full lovemaking session.

FEMALE AROUSAL

Male sexuality is pretty straightforward – men are usually quickly aroused and have no trouble reaching orgasm. But the female orgasm is more elusive. Most women have a slower and more complex sexual response and their orgasm depends on many factors, including how secure they feel and what their partner does to stimulate them.

INDUCING ORGASM

Surveys show that penetration is the least likely way to induce orgasm in a woman. That's because in most positions the penis doesn't touch the clitoris – the little pea-shaped organ that hides under a hood of skin between the labia and above the entrance to the vagina. The clitoris is the epicentre of female pleasure, but that doesn't mean you should make a beeline for it – touch this highly sensitive organ

only after plenty of foreplay
has made both labia and
clitoris swell with blood,
much as the penis becomes
erect. This is the signal that
a woman is truly ready for
the climax.

SOFTLY, SOFTLY

Before you even touch her
genitals, arouse your partner
with kisses – mouth to mouth
and all over her body – and

by cradling her in your arms
and stroking her skin. The
first genital contact can be a
light brushing of the hand
across the pubic hair. Read
her response and when she is
ready, explore with your
fingers inside her vulva.

The best way to give a
woman an orgasm is with oral
sex (cunnilingus). Spend as
much time on it as it takes
before you penetrate her and

have your own first orgasm. Once she knows you are prepared to lavish unlimited attention on her she will relax and be able to lose herself in the sheer bliss of what she is feeling – and there's nothing more likely to boost a man's ego than making his partner come in this way.

Try a session where she undresses completely but you stay dressed (wearing something non-constricting like tracksuit bottoms) until you have given her an orgasm.

Many women confound the 'complex response' theory by being able to make themselves come really quite quickly – often as fast as men can – when they masturbate or use a vibrator. This is usually as a result of a combination of being in the right mood and knowing exactly which parts of themselves to touch and how. Ask your partner to show you what she does to herself – then try to do it yourself under her guidance.

109

MALE MASTURBATION

You can learn a lot about how to handle your partner's penis by watching him masturbate. And then you can improve on his repertoire by adding imaginative variations of your own.

IS HE CIRCUMCISED OR NOT?

Circumcision is often carried out on male babies for reasons of religion or tradition. It is the surgical removal of the foreskin, so a circumcised adult penis lacks the hood of skin that covers the glans (tip) of a flaccid uncircumcised penis. Surveys suggest that most women prefer the neater look of circumcised men, but find it easier to masturbate an uncircumcised penis.

In the US there is a movement among circumcised men to 'regrow' their foreskins by exercising and with weights. Some men say that the unsheathed glans loses its sensitivity as it rubs against clothing, robbing them of the more exquisite sexual sensations.

GETTING IT RIGHT

It can be daunting for a man to have his partner try to give him an erection by direct manipulation. Pressure to perform is never a turn-on. So wait, and don't handle his penis until it's erect and aching to be touched:

- Make your movements confident, firm and leisurely. Give him the feeling you are totally in control and in no hurry
- If he is circumcised, concentrate on the shaft, moving the penile skin up towards the glans then back down again
- Tune into his needs while you are masturbating him. Tantalize him by changing the rhythm or speed as well

as by varying the angle and pressure you use

- Try drumming your fingers on the shaft as if you were playing the flute

THE TECHNIQUE

1 Brush the flat of your palm along the insides of his legs, over his balls and quickly and lightly up the shaft, hardly touching the tip. Do this several times, increasing the pressure. His penis will strain up to meet your hand.

2 'Weigh' his penis in your hand. Lift it up and let it drop back – smack – on to his belly. Watch it bounce. Repeat.

3 Hold the shaft firmly in your hand and squeeze repeatedly, first very gently and then more firmly, as you passionately kiss his mouth.

4 Walk your fingers in small mischievous steps up the shaft and very lightly tickle the tip as it rises to meet you.

5 If he is uncircumcised, hold the penis in your hand and make a snugly fitting circle with your forefinger and thumb just below the glans. Slowly pull the foreskin down. Stop. Squeeze. Raise the foreskin again. Take your time. Steadily build a rhythm.

6 Towards the end, keep up the pressure and speed coolly and with control – he needs no distractions now – and when you feel his body tense in advance orgasm, hold on and carry through, not stopping until he subsides.

THE TESTICLES

In sex play, the testicles are often neglected, perhaps since everyone knows they are very pain-sensitive – but they also respond well to stimulation. Many men adore having them caressed and licked.

HANDLING THE TESTICLES

1 First, take a good look. They swell slightly with arousal, and move under the skin, creating an effect like waves out at sea. Just before ejaculation, they tighten and rise up under the penis.

2 Pay attention to his inner thighs. Stroke them fleetingly with the palms of your hands, then push them apart and breathe hot air on them, barely touching them with your lips. Nuzzle his balls and trace the 'seam' between them with your tongue. Then playfully lick one then the other from below, working round the sides to the top.

3 Pay attention to the perineum. Massage it with little walking steps with your fingers, pressing quite firmly, then swoop into feathery strokes all over the balls, alternating with cupping them in your hand and 'testing their weight'.

4 With a firm tongue, lick vigorously and repeatedly from the upper corner of his thigh towards the point where penis and scrotum join. Then lick the testicle nearest to you with the same firm motion, occasionally 'accidentally' straying on to the root of the erect penis.

5 After licking his testicles all over with little flicks, probing between them with the tip of your tongue to define their shape, nibble them with your lips, lick salaciously with the flat of your tongue, and gradually take one or both balls in your mouth. Use your lips and tongue only to manoeuvre them – keep your teeth covered by your lips.

114

Oral Sex

The intimacy of mouth-to-genital contact is a powerful turn-on, both physically and emotionally. Physically, the super-sensitive tongue is a versatile instrument of pleasure for both sexes. From an emotional point of view, a certain level of intimacy, trust and lack of inhibition is required to surrender fully to the delights of oral sex.

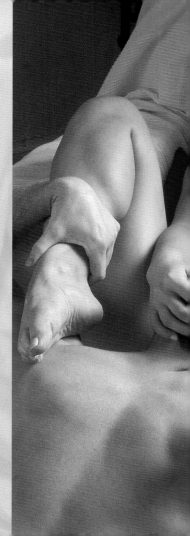

CUNNILINGUS

More women experience an orgasm every time with oral sex than through any other form of sexual congress. This is because of the exquisite pleasure that the tongue can deliver by means of slippery, feathery or firm flicking movements over and around the clitoris. These tongue-generated orgasms are also generally more powerful than those given by the fingers.

THE MOST COMFORTABLE POSITION

She lies on her back on the bed with her legs splayed and her knees up towards her stomach. You lie on your front with your head between her legs, supporting her thighs with your hands, which you can also use to brush her pubic hair out of the way and gently part her labia. Another good position

118

is for her to lean back in a comfortable chair, with you sitting on the floor in front of her on a cushion.

LICKING TIPS

Every woman's vaginal juices taste different – salty, nutty or sweet. This is usually part of why you love her, but if you're worried about first-time hygiene, make having a bath or shower together part of your erotic menu.

Be very gentle and wait until she is fully aroused before making contact with the clitoris. The whole of the vulva will swell and flush, and the clitoris may well appear red and swollen from inside its hood.

A respondent in one survey said he plays what he calls 'the alphabet game' – writing capital letters with his tongue very slowly over his partner's open vulva, barely touching the clitoris as he passes it.

Get your partner to help you by communicating what

119

feels best. Rather than have her say: 'Up a bit, down a bit,' ask her to describe where she would like to be licked next by imagining her vulva as a clock face. Six o'clock, found at the opening of the vagina, and twelve o'clock, right above the clitoris, are particularly sensitive areas.

Probe into her vagina with your tongue, then try gentle firm pressure all over the vulva, letting your tongue 'dance'. A repeated light rhythmic flicking across the clitoris will usually have the effect of inducing the tension that releases into orgasm.

Many women find the clitoris is too sensitive to touch after they come. Ask what she likes – often this is the best time for penetration.

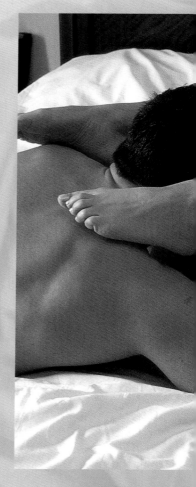

FELLATIO

Cleopatra was honoured with the title 'the great swallower'. Her enemies told of her fellating dozens of soldiers in her army in one night. If you haven't swallowed semen before, masturbate or fellate your partner to orgasm and dip your finger in the semen as it squirts out of his urethra. It feels warm and may taste nutty, salty or sweet, depending on what he has been eating and drinking. If he isn't well, it may taste bitter. The best time to swallow it is on ejaculation, as it becomes cloudy and viscous as it cools.

LICK AND SUCK
During fellatio, the woman, not the man, should be in control. How deeply she takes him into her mouth is down to her. In any case, some penises are too big for this and some mouths too small.

123

There are plenty of more enjoyable and sophisticated ways to give fellatio than simply thrusting in the mouth. Use your imagination...

THE TECHNIQUE

Be prepared to move around your partner's body as you lick and suck his penis, so you can enjoy it from every angle.
1 Nuzzle the shaft with the inside of your lips and apply pressure with the flat of your tongue as your mouth moves up and down towards the tip. Start at one side, move up and down the penis on top of him, then continue with the other side. Be energetic and thorough.
2 Hold the penis in your hand and, lubricating it with plenty of saliva and/or almond oil, masturbate it slowly, lavishly licking and tickling the tip with your tongue. Keep up well-lubricated flowing movements, alternating

all the time between hands and tongue, so he hardly knows where the sensation is coming from. Let your mouth follow your hand in a smooth rhythm.
3 Now suck the tip of the penis with greedy sucking noises and lots of saliva, moving your hand rapidly

and lightly up and down
the shaft, and tickling the
opening of the urethra with
the tip of your tongue.
4 Feel his whole body tense,
then spasm as he comes.
Some men need you to carry
on licking and sucking
through several spasms, but
with others, the glans

becomes so sensitive that they
can't bear contact any longer.
5 If you are not going to
swallow the ejaculate, try
letting it squirt on to your
lips and fingers and
massaging it into the still
throbbing penis until
ejaculation stops and the
movement subsides.

INDEX

ACKNOWLEDGEMENTS

Photography Peter Everard Smith

All photographs © Octopus Publishing Group/Peter Everard Smith